Frozen Fawn

Frozen Fawn

poems by Ally McGregor

~2026~

Frozen Fawn

Editor-in-chief
Eric Morago

Operations Associate
Shelly Holder

Associate Editors
Mackensi E. Green
Allysa Murray
Rob Sturma
Ellen Webre

Editor Emeritus
Michael Miller

Cover art
Alice Snow

Cover design
Eric Morago

Book design
Michael Wada

Moon Tide logo design
Abraham Gomez

Frozen Fawn
is published by Moon Tide Press

Moon Tide Press
6709 Washington Ave. #9297
Whittier, CA 90608
www.moontidepress.com

FIRST EDITION

Printed in the United States of America

ISBN # 978-1-957799-96-4

Contents

Freeze

Fawn

Fight

Content Warning

The following poems reference potentially triggering subjects,
including misogyny, acephobia, ableism,
self-harm, gore, & suicide.

Freeze

Liquid Nitrogen

Who would say that spots live and help one live? Ink, blood smell. I do not know what ink I would use that would want to leave its track in such forms. I respect its wishes and I will do what I can to flee from myself worlds, Inked worlds—land free and mine.

—Frida Kahlo

Decry I'm cryogenic—coldly comatose—so clinical—how could
anything be this frigid—you say: disturbingly uncompelled by
the heat of flesh—I say: impervious—you're dragging your tongue
over lascivious lips—panting—moaning—probing—stroking—
except now the lips are popsicle sticks—gotcha—innocent,
really, how you fell for that—cute, even—what about a lithesome
abdomen writhing under you—indecent indentation—indication
of somewhere lower—"forbidden"—that's surely enticing—or is
it too predictable—boring—you think I've seen nothing—but
I'm quite the voyeur—you'll have to do more to surprise me—
please surprise me—I'm terribly bored—get on with it—there's
only so many positions—so many paddles & ribbons—aren't you
tired—I could share my cerulean with you—there's something
exhilarating about apathy—come, let us be hypothermic
together—when you thaw, I'll still be here—the written word as
salacious as oral—a marshmallow dipped in liquid nitrogen just as
sweet—I suppose you're right to fear the ink—the crunch of
cracked teeth

Roses Are Blue

The blue and the wind, the blue wind.

— Nadja

Winter splits the lonely snail's shell—
        & though what once was broken
can never be whole, I repair
        her home with lacquer & gold.
A fish with human legs sleeps
        suspended in the frozen lake—
frost crystallizing her vulva.
        I blow hot breaths over her frigid body,
but she melts along with the ice—
        puddle cupped in my shivering palms.
I fill a glass with her & gently
        close the refrigerator.
A single rose blooms in the snow—
        stem swaying in the blue wind.
I pluck her from the cold
        to swaddle her, yet I cannot prevent
her withering in my arms.
        I place her petals in a picture frame—
straightening the corners,
        sighing in reverence.
She is sovereign over my mantel,
        but the door left ajar
brings gusts of cerulean again.
        Shattered glass,
smothered fire—
        answer me.
Why do I preserve
        what's already dead?
The swallow of an already-dissolved pill—
        the maddened mind that stills—

kindness that kills—
emptiness that fills.
I suspect there's something sacred
about a sad paradox—
the intimacy of contradiction—
a stubbornly irresolute will.

Lunacy

Caught by breasts by hands and by hair / never yielded herself whole / so mad of lichens lost / like a needle in moss / by all the ends urgent false / I have turned you you have woven me

—Valentine Penrose

Full moons transmute
feminine hair to bones to fur
the wilderness of a follicle
stripping pigment
grey as spoiled snow
corruption of purity
construct of constraint
howl with the wind
make platonic love
until your voice gives
extended claws rip holes in time
each year month hour reduced to lines
yet silver severs beastly vessels
inquisitor's blade of the rational
cave of folly collapsed
permanent imprisonment
for wits of difference
lycanthrope devolves to lichen
mingled with the espionage of moss
hiding bodies underground
the new moon of a dirt mound.

Brain Freeze

I ceased menstruating at the time...I was transforming my blood into comprehensive energy—masculine and feminine, microcosmic and macrocosmic—and also into a wine which was drunk by the moon and the sun.

— Leonora Carrington

I see / her /
strapped in the sanitarium

every day I make-up my face
to conceal the blue circles

under my eyes
I find them beautiful

duochrome twilight

from staying awake
for three days straight

/ write /paint / pace / sit / stare / jump /
/ run / crawl / cry / laugh / die / live /

but I can't be sent home from work

/ again /

when playful shadows
in my periphery show me

all the wounds
/ I! Could! Do! /

voices in my head

a cacophony of reapers

who adore sanguine weddings / consummate scythe to skin /
my psychiatrist has a sworn duty

to keep me “preserved”
/ we disagree on the matter /

so I become a sculpture

crystalline ice
how could anyone be disturbed

by a frozen face chiseled

into a / tolerable / smile?

they let us carry around

our own icepicks now

isn’t / that / nice?

I got mine online to keep in my purse

/ blood frosted to sapphires /

/ brain a raspberry sorbet /

jamming it into my socket

whenever I begin to warm

ugly bruise of compliance

yet surely / sedation /

by my hand
is better than / obliteration / by yours?

If the Icepick Slips / the Prude Loses Her Virginity

In If/When one player writes the first half of a proposition, the second player, having no idea what the first has written, adds the conclusion.

— Penelope Rosemont

If the snowman's erect / wait for the immaculate conception

If centrifugal force is the cure / the DSM-5 is the bible

If the blizzard's a syringe / hysterical women weep gasoline

If the concupiscence fails / the sedated chaste will copulate

If the hydrotherapy freezes / the puritans knot another noose

If the atheist prays / read the error in Fahrenheit

If there had been no asylums / there'd be so many delicious flames

If the maiden wears rouge / the cervix will regurgitate the chewed carrot

If the moon is nude / roll gently back & forth

If the pocket watch sighs / the snow will fall red

When the sun starts to die / drill holes in the head

The Black Hole

Into the red velvet of your belly / Into the blackness of your secret cries / I have ventured / And the earth spins round humming...

— Joyce Mansour

I call my Unconscious *The Black Hole*

because it warps space-time

wrinkling the fabric of the universe

or perhaps less melodramatically

the fabric of me

I'm also the star that ventures too close

consciousness swirling

an accretion disk

rapidly spinning inward

past the event horizon

no cosmologist

can see inside

just as no psychiatrist

knows my mind

it's different than dissociation

I promise

dissociation is floaty

a helium balloon bobbing
above a skull

tethered to vertebrae with string

but this   this is dense

gravity splayed

like a weighted blanket   hugging

my back as I lay

face-down
in sub-zero snow

fine   I concede
it's *meditation*
but forgive me

for not knowing that fact

when I was in middle school

not when I needed to name

this entity that let words   escape

to paper   during class

obfuscated metaphors   to document

the bullies' bruises

on my ribs

to explain   my death drive

my distorted   pleasure principle

somewhere cold & safe to hide

ketamine infusions

sucked me deeper

revealed to me what I know now

that this black hole
is chromatic

each letter of the alphabet

the very construct

of language itself

a different hue

& bruises freeze when B is blue

& abuse is velvet

when A is red

& L is yellow

when light is liberated

please excuse

the scientific inaccuracies I'm aware light cannot flee

a black hole

but mine gives me nothing but *colorful brightness*

blinding freedom
be jealous, if you must

Don't Tap the Glass

"You wish my breast to be a snowball," said the young woman. "Very well, I agree. But what will you do for me in return?"

— Simone Kahn

I watch you from the snow globe
that sits upon your antique bookshelf—
leaving fingerprints trailed along the glass
as I circle the same rotation over & over—
trudging through plastic snow
that erases my footsteps,
past evergreen trees whose needles
never fall, a cottage in the woods
whose door never opens.

You look up from your bed,
bored by the book you're reading.

Walking to me,
you stroke the glass
& I shiver—though it isn't cold
under this dome.

With your muffled voice,
you propose we play a game—
one of echoes.

You snap your fingers
& my dress lifts
over my head.

I'm naked as you hold the globe
closer to your glossy eyes—
peering deeper as we
simultaneously speak:

"The blue pallor	*Valor*
of your gills	*fills*
undulates ache—	*opaque*
untouchable places,	*faces*
deity of antifreeze—	*please*
you know I won't	*don't*
lift my palm to slap—	*tap*
cease your fearful sigh	*my*
& let me admire your frosted grass."	*glass.*

You drop me in defiance
& I shatter—
glass piercing
my breasts.

Rolling me over
with your polished shoe—
you pull a shard out of my flesh—

bleeding, breathing—
is this how drowning feels?

Blood vessels collapsing—
body thrashing—

I think, darling,
this is the rapture—

I see light particles
swirling in the air—

or is this just the way
oxygen becomes variegated
when it explodes
in the space between us?

Fawn

Coffee Stain in the Shape of an Antler

The principle used in many processes of surrealist painting is to make a stain—by chance, or automatically, as we say, and then to look into it and see what forms it suggests to our imagination, and finally to develop these forms into a completed work of art.

— Ithell Colquhoun

I
esp-
ecially
It's   see the
the   penis
Elec-   envy
tra   here—
Com-   the   But
plex   tension   I have
of   between   a good
it   the   relation-   &
all—   ego   ship   the
you   &   with   rep-
know,   silly   my   ression!
the   id.   mother.   I must
castration—   be
see the   stuck
curvature?   there—
It's   repressed
common   so much
This   in us   I have
part   manic-   no
is   depress-   sexuality
the   ives.   at all,
matri-   We love   they'd
cide.   to just   say.
spontan-
eously
regress,
I guess.

Napkin note:
I don't know if this looks
much like an antler.
I've never seen one
in-person before.

Experimental Research: On the Mental Fortitude & Sexual Apathy of the Object: The Fawn with a Dozen Eyes

Questions:

1. Is it diurnal or nocturnal? 2. Is it favorable toward love? 3. Is it suitable for metamorphoses? 4. What is its spatial location with respect to the individual? 5. What epoch does it correspond to? 6. What happens if it is submerged in water? 7. in milk? 8. in vinegar? 9. in urine? 10. in alcohol? 11. in mercury? 12. What element does it correspond to? 13. What philosophical system does it belong to? 14. What disease does it remind you of? 15. What sex is it? 16. With which historical personage may it be identified? 17. How does it die? 18. What must it meet up with on a dissecting table for it to look beautiful? 19. With what two objects would one wish to see it in the desert? 20. On which spot of the nude body of a woman would you place it? 21. and if the woman were sleeping? 22. and if she were dead? 23. What sign of the Zodiac does it correspond to? 24. Where on an armchair would you place it? 25. Where on a bed would you place it? 26. What crime does it correspond to?

—Denise Bellon, Gala Dalí, Nusch Eluard, Yolande Oliviero

1. Nocturnal 2. Highly unfavorable 3. It seems distraught by the notion that any of its features would appeal to potential mates, thus it is unlikely to metamorphosize physically, but perhaps may metaphysically 4. They are one & the same 5. 1924 6. It breathes 7. It suckles 8. It pickles 9. It vomits, then faints—fearing contamination in an obsessive-compulsive manner 10. No effect 11. It maddens 12. Water 13. Existentialism bordering on Nihilism, depending on the hour 14. Bipolar Disorder 15. Femme 16. André Breton 17. It begs to but won't 18. With TMS, Ketamine, ECT & an icepick 19. With paper & glue so that it may cocoon 20. Her womb so that it may reverse its birth 21. Her brain so that it may walk her dreams

22. Her eyes so that it may collect them 23. Pisces, but it will lie & say Aquarius 24. On the psychiatrist's lap 25. In the center, alone 26. Identity theft.

Frottage

...What sort of hope do you place in love...the hope never to recognize (for myself) any raison d'être outside love...Would you, willingly or not, sacrifice your freedom for it? Have you done so?...I reject that two lovers might be in contradiction on a topic as serious as love. I do not wish to be free...Love as I conceive it has no barrier to cross, no cause to betray.

— Suzanne Muzard

The surrealist art of duplication—
of rubbing pencil, etc. on paper draped
over an object to replicate its form.

I never asked for the leaf's consent
when I severed it from the tree—
suffocating it with the manufactured,
pulpy corpse of its own mother—
artificial green crayon crafting
a copy of its unnecessary demise.

It's only polysemic justice that the Universe
presses its crotch against me now.

Is this love?
The dominance—
the helplessness—
the one-sided sexual gratification.

The way the leaf decomposes
once the artist discards it,
we, too, shall—
alone & violated—
return to earth.

Experimental Research Part Two: On What the Fawn with a Dozen Eyes Hates, Loves, Wants, & Fears

Surrealist Inquiry:

1.) What do you hate most?
2.) What do you love most?
3.) What do you want most?
4.) What do you fear most?

— Emmy Bridgwater, Ithell Colquhoun, Iréne Hamoir, and Edith Rimmington

1.) The uncanny nature of faces, the buzz of light bulbs, headaches from huffing scented candles, touching mold on wet dishes, myself, mouth sounds, anything bitter, guns, empty apologies, lying, André Breton's neurotic quest for love, the persistence of scabs, how damn difficult it is to die when you want to, bodily fluids, mushy fruit, hallucinations, ticking clocks, the infantilizing and humiliating ritual of collecting my virgin blood into a vial each month to prove I'm a *"real"* asexual.

2.) Superfluous adjectives, assonance, the way you can swallow the moon without chewing, duality, phallic silicone in nefarious places, poetry, caramel macchiatos, the whimsy of loneliness, kaleidoscopes, smooth jazz, the color pink, Paris, hypomania, blue curaçao cocktails, André Breton's infuriating brilliance, the Carrington Event, mannequins & dolls, dog clickers, typewriters, vampires, the number 5, surrealism, soft blankets, slug sex.

3.) To be taxidermy—stuffed and sewn up—propped in a museum for passersby to marvel at the ironic history of fawns. *Oh, the poor thing, it had so many eyes, too many indeed. It must have seen so much it shouldn't have. There is such a thing as being too perceptive. At some point, the magnifying glass becomes the laser beam.*

4.) Crowds, public speaking, spiders, open windows, the multiverse, pregnancy, new medications, failed suicide attempts, churches, embarrassment, fame, surprises, pleurisy, nuclear war, being evil without knowing it, total silence, telepathy, pain, the dark, the patriarchy, eye-contact, unlocked doors, being touched, love, misspeaking, high-magnitude earthquakes, the idea of an afterlife, immortality, being forgotten, being remembered.

Spell for Invisibility

He saw in me what he wanted to see, but he didn't really see me.

— Jacqueline Lamba

I'm visiting from another plane of existence

held captive by the way light refuses

to fracture around my form

my body blending into wallpaper

printed with ferns & flowers

as the barista calls

another name that isn't mine

because I have no name

not here

yet, you insist you see me

squinting from your table at the faint

outline of a woman

or, at least, mostly one

some days, I am more carcass

other days I am nothing but a coward

pleading placating sedating

in that order

as my hooves un-knot a noose

hanging above

a mantel

today I feel quite like a flank of bubbles

unable to pop

you try to

with confident fingers

but I remain afloat clean & soapy

when all I seek is the warmth
of earthly release

everyone else seems to enjoy but me

perhaps you should visit

my dimension instead

where bullets don't pass

straight through me

shoot me & I'll bleed for you

under the glow

of two moons

a parallax I'll bloom

by fluttering your eyes shut

don't open them

this spell is ephemeral

my soft, shimmering translucence

will return to matte flesh

no longer an enigma of luminescence

when I reveal my corporeality

will you promise to stay with me

if I still speak in riddles

what has white spots

even in snowfall

that shivers in pain

from your cruel
& violent hand

yet still licks your wrist?

Fight

You Are Ardently Invited to a Romantic Dinner with, Sincerely Yours, the Bourgeoisie

Purity! Purity! Purity! / I am happy! Happy! / PASCAL and NIETZCHE! And their shouts / And their PRIDE! AND ABOVE ALL! / Oh, above all / THEIR PURITY! AND BEETHOVEN... / AND even MORE! AND THEIR IMMORTALITY... / PURITY! PRIDE! PAIN! ...AND YOU, THE PROLETARIAT? /...YOU AND I, WE SHALL PERISH!

— Fanny Beznos

The napkins on your laps are delicately embroidered with skulls /

you wipe your mouths of our membranes / splattered /

on porcelain plates / we're splayed on the table / bodies

once concealed by silver domes / revealed / spectacle / the clink

of champagne glasses / the exchange of roses / as you stick

expensive forks into our flanks / we freeze / you chew /

we plead with doe eyes / you swallow / you reach to cut

out our tongues / & we bite / & bite / your teeth sinking

into our flesh /

our teeth sinking / into your bones / screams /

knocking over candles /

as we thrash / the fat in your bodies / beautiful fuel /

flames licking you all over

/ understanding lust / how erotic hot flesh is /

when everything burns / not caring about the morality of arson /

or the vile taste of you as you settle in our stomachs / brave /

as we regenerate our legs

Acknowledgment

Thank you to the original surrealists for forever inspiring me both in art and in life, even one hundred years after the first Manifesto of Surrealism. I hope to continue to expand upon your brilliant and radical work with the goal of a more inclusive revolution of the mind and liberation for all. I especially want to thank the women surrealists of the past, who many only viewed as muses. Your work is just as important. You are powerful artists. You are not invisible. I see you, and through the wormhole of time, I'm holding your hands.

Works Cited

All epigraphs used (with the exception of the quote by Jacqueline Lamba, which comes from an article titled "Jacqueline Lamba: From Darkness with Light" by Weinstein Gallery, Inc.) are from *Surrealist Women: An International Anthology,* edited with introductions by Penelope Rosemont. Below are the works' individual titles, first lines, or headings if they are untitled, and corresponding translators' names when applicable:

"From Her Journal," Frida Kahlo, translated from the Spanish by Hayden Herrera

"The Blue Wind," Nadja, also known as Léona Camille Ghislaine D., translated from the French by Richard Howard

"To A Woman To A Path," Valentine Penrose, translated from the French by Roland Penrose and Valentine Penrose

"Down Below," Leonora Carrington, excerpts from VVV no. 4 (New York, 1944, Chicago: Black Swan Press, 1983), translated from the French by Victor Llona

"Surrealist Games: If/When," explanation by Penelope Rosemont

"Into The Red Velvet," Joyce Mansour, translated from the French by Peter Wood and Guy Flandre

"Surrealist Text: This Took Place In Springtime…," Simone Kahn, translated from the French by Guy Ducornet

"The Mantic Stain: Surrealism And Automatism," Ithell Colquhoun, from *Enquiry,* London: October-November, 1949

"Experimental Research: On The Irrational Knowledge Of The Object: The Crystal Ball Of The Seers," Denise Bellon, Gala Dalí, Nusch Eluard, and Yolande Oliviero, translated from the French by Myrna Bell Rochester

"On Love: Reply To An Inquiry," Suzanne Muzard, translated from the French by Guy Ducornet

"Surrealist Inquiry: What Do You Hate Most?," Emmy Bridgwater, Ithell Colquhoun, Iréne Hamoir, and Edith Rimmington, translated from the French by Penelope Rosemont

"Purity! Purity! Purity!," Fanny Beznos, translated from the French by Myrna Bell Rochester

Also Available from Moon Tide Press

The Ground Never Lets Go, Liz Marlow (2026)
Afterburn, Rebecca Evans (2026)
Not So Fast, Sarah McMahon (2026)
The Elephant of Surprise, Charles Harper Webb (2026)
Outliving Michael, Steven Reigns (2025)
Prayers With a Side of Cash, Kathleen Florence (2025)
Somewhere, a Playground, Rich Ferguson (2025)
The Tautology of Water, Giovanni Boskovich (2025)
Take Care, Mark Danowsky (2025)
Dilapitatia, Kelly Gray (2025)
Reluctant Prophets, J.D. Isip (2025)
Enormous Blue Umbrella, Donna Hilbert (2025)
Sky Leaning Toward Winter, Terri Niccum (2024)
Living the Sundown: A Caregiving Memoir, G. Murray Thomas (2024)
Figure Study, Kathryn de Lancellotti (2024)
Suffer for This: Love, Sex, Marriage, & Rock 'N' Roll,
  Victor D. Infante (2024)
What Blooms in the Dark, Emily J. Mundy (2024)
Fable, Bryn Wickerd (2024)
Diamond Bars 2, David A. Romero (2024)
Safe Handling, Rebecca Evans (2024)
More Jerkumstances: New & Selected Poems, Barbara Eknoian (2024)
Dissection Day, Ally McGregor (2023)
He's a Color Until He's Not, Christian Hanz Lozada (2023)
The Language of Fractions, Nicelle Davis (2023)
Paradise Anonymous, Oriana Ivy (2023)
Now You Are a Missing Person, Susan Hayden (2023)
Maze Mouth, Brian Sonia-Wallace (2023)
Tangled by Blood, Rebecca Evans (2023)
Another Way of Loving Death, Jeremy Ra (2023)
Kissing the Wound, J.D. Isip (2023)
Feed It to the River, Terhi K. Cherry (2022)
*Beat Not Beat: An Anthology of California Poets Screwing
  on the Beat and Post-Beat Tradition* (2022)
*When There Are Nine: Poems Celebrating the Life and
  Achievements of Ruth Bader Ginsburg* (2022)

The Knife Thrower's Daughter, Terri Niccum (2022)
2 Revere Place, Aruni Wijesinghe (2022)
Here Go the Knives, Kelsey Bryan-Zwick (2022)
Trumpets in the Sky, Jerry Garcia (2022)
Threnody, Donna Hilbert (2022)
A Burning Lake of Paper Suns, Ellen Webre (2021)
Instructions for an Animal Body, Kelly Gray (2021)
*Head *V* Heart: New & Selected Poems*, Rob Sturma (2021)
Sh!t Men Say to Me: A Poetry Anthology in Response to Toxic Masculinity (2021)
Flower Grand First, Gustavo Hernandez (2021)
Everything is Radiant Between the Hates, Rich Ferguson (2020)
When the Pain Starts: Poetry as Sequential Art, Alan Passman (2020)
This Place Could Be Haunted If I Didn't Believe in Love, Lincoln McElwee (2020)
Impossible Thirst, Kathryn de Lancellotti (2020)
Lullabies for End Times, Jennifer Bradpiece (2020)
Crabgrass World, Robin Axworthy (2020)
Contortionist Tongue, Dania Ayah Alkhouli (2020)
The only thing that makes sense is to grow, Scott Ferry (2020)
Dead Letter Box, Terri Niccum (2019)
Tea and Subtitles: Selected Poems 1999-2019, Michael Miller (2019)
At the Table of the Unknown, Alexandra Umlas (2019)
The Book of Rabbits, Vince Trimboli (2019)
Everything I Write Is a Love Song to the World, David McIntire (2019)
Letters to the Leader, HanaLena Fennel (2019)
Darwin's Garden, Lee Rossi (2019)
Dark Ink: A Poetry Anthology Inspired by Horror (2018)
Drop and Dazzle, Peggy Dobreer (2018)
Junkie Wife, Alexis Rhone Fancher (2018)
The Moon, My Lover, My Mother, & the Dog, Daniel McGinn (2018)
Lullaby of Teeth: An Anthology of Southern California Poetry (2017)
Angels in Seven, Michael Miller (2016)
A Likely Story, Robbi Nester (2014)
Embers on the Stairs, Ruth Bavetta (2014)

The Green of Sunset, John Brantingham (2013)
The Savagery of Bone, Timothy Matthew Perez (2013)
The Silence of Doorways, Sharon Venezio (2013)
Cosmos: An Anthology of Southern California Poetry (2012)
Straws and Shadows, Irena Praitis (2012)
In the Lake of Your Bones, Peggy Dobreer (2012)
I Was Building Up to Something, Susan Davis (2011)
Hopeless Cases, Michael Kramer (2011)
One World, Gail Newman (2011)
What We Ache For, Eric Morago (2010)
Now and Then, Lee Mallory (2009)
Pop Art: An Anthology of Southern California Poetry (2009)
In the Heaven of Never Before, Carine Topal (2008)
A Wild Region, Kate Buckley (2008)
Carving in Bone: An Anthology of Orange County Poetry (2007)
Kindness from a Dark God, Ben Trigg (2007)
A Thin Strand of Lights, Ricki Mandeville (2006)
Sleepyhead Assassins, Mindy Nettifee (2006)
Tide Pools: An Anthology of Orange County Poetry (2006)
Lost American Nights: Lyrics & Poems, Michael Ubaldini (2006)

Patrons

Moon Tide Press would like to thank the following people for their support in helping publish the finest poetry from the Southern California region. To sign up as a patron, visit www.moontidepress.com or send an email to publisher@moontidepress.com.

Anonymous
Robin Axworthy
Conner Brenner
Nicole Connolly
Bill Cushing
Susan Davis
Kristen Baum DeBeasi
Peggy Dobreer
Kate Gale
Dennis Gowans
Alexis Rhone Fancher
HanaLena Fennel
Half Off Books & Brad T. Cox
Donna Hilbert
Jim & Vicky Hoggatt
Michael Kramer
Ron Koertge &
Bianca Richards
Gary Jacobelly
Ray & Christi Lacoste
Jeffery Lewis
Zachary & Tammy Locklin
Lincoln McElwee
David McIntire
José Enrique Medina
Michael Miller &
Rachanee Srisavasdi
Michelle & Robert Miller
Ronny & Richard Morago
Terri Niccum
Andrew November
Jeremy Ra
Luke & Mia Salazar
Jennifer Smith
Roger Sponder
Andrew Turner
Rex Wilder
Mariano Zaro
Wes Bryan Zwick

www.ingramcontent.com/pod-product-compliance
Lightning Source LLC
LaVergne TN
LVHW011053110826
845149LV00015B/3484